Little Mitchie

FLIES THAT SEE IN SLOW MOTION

TRACY VONDER BRINK

CREATING YOUNG NONFICTION READERS

Little Mitchie books spark curiosity and support early nonfiction reading for students in Grades 2-3. Designed to build vocabulary, support second language learners, and prepare readers for middle-grade content, each book includes helpful tips for parents and educators to build confidence and deepen understanding of the world.

TIPS FOR READING NONFICTION WITH BEGINNING READERS

Talk about Nonfiction

Begin by explaining that nonfiction books give us information that is true. The book will be organized around a specific topic or idea, and we may learn new facts through reading.

Look at the Parts

Most nonfiction books have helpful features. Our *Little Mitchie* titles include color photographs and graphic aids, a table of contents, a glossary, and an index. Share the purpose of these features with your reader.

Color Photos and Graphic Aids

A lot of information can be found by "reading" photos, charts, maps, and other graphic aids found within nonfiction texts. Help your reader learn more about the different ways information can be displayed.

Table of Contents

Located at the front of the book, this list shows the big ideas within the text and the page numbers where they can be found.

Glossary

Located at the back of the book, the glossary defines key words and phrases that are related to the topic. These words and phrases can be found in the text in colored type.

Index

Located at the back of the book, an index is an alphabetical list of topics and the page numbers where they can be found.

With a little help and guidance about reading nonfiction, you can feel good about introducing a young reader to the world of *Little Mitchie* nonfiction books.

Little Mitchie is an imprint of:

Mitchell Lane
PUBLISHERS

2001 SW 31st Avenue
Hallandale, FL 33009
mitchelllanepub.com

First Edition, 2027.

Author: Tracy Vonder Brink
Designer: Jen Bowers
Editor: Tricia Hoffman

Library of Congress Cataloging-in-Publication Data
Title: Flies That See in Slow Motion / by Tracy Vonder Brink

Description: Hallandale, FL :
Mitchell Lane Publishers, [2027]

Identifiers:
ISBN 979-8-89260-885-5 (library bound)
ISBN 979-8-89260-988-3 (eBook)

Library of Congress Control Number: 2026936381

PHOTO CREDITS
Shutterstock: cover, p.1 ©2023 DiTiara Mobilegraphy, p.5 ©2018 Maren Winter, p.6, 22 ©2023 Sri Handoko Duto Pamugkas, p.9 ©2017 Komsan Loonprom, p.10, 22 ©2019 Cornel Constantin, p.11, 22 ©2018 Tran The Ngoc, p.12 ©2024 Hady abobakr, p.14–15 ©2023 Master1305, p.17 ©2011 Cathy Keifer, p.18 ©2019 fukume, p.21 ©2024 Fredi Ahmeda Jaya

TABLE OF CONTENTS

Chapter One

EYE SEE YOU

You try to swat a fly, but it zooms away every time. How? It sees faster than you can move!

MIGHTY MOMENT

Male flies can spot light bouncing off females' wings. Scientists think this helps male flies track down mates.

Vision is one of a fly's important **senses**. Flies use at least half of their brains to help them see. Their vision helps them escape danger and find food and mates.

Chapter Two

SEEING IS BELIEVING

Each of a person's eyes has one **lens**. Flies are different. They have **compound** eyes. Each compound eye has thousands of lenses.

The lenses cover the whole eye. This lets flies see in almost every direction at the same time. They don't need to turn their eyes or heads to see something coming.

MIGHTY MOMENT

Most flies also have three simple eyes on top of their heads. These eyes are much smaller and only help pick up light.

All eyes work by changing light into **nerve** signals that go to the brain. Then, the brain uses the signals to figure out what the person or animal is looking at. Flies' eyes and brains do this much faster than a person's.

Being able to take in images fast changes the way flies see things. To them, it looks like things are moving in slow **motion**!

MIGHTY MOMENT

If a fly could watch a movie, it would look like clicking through a set of pictures in a slideshow.

Chapter Three

UP, UP, AND AWAY

Flies are able to see shapes, but their eyes can't **focus** the way a person's can. That's part of why they zoom off. They can't tell exactly what's coming toward them or how dangerous it is.

MIGHTY MOMENT

Flies see some colors. They can also see some kinds of light you can't. Picking up on colors and light helps them find food.

Flies don’t spend time trying to figure out what it is that’s coming toward them. Any motion causes their brains to make them fly away.

Chapter Four

FABULOUS FLIES

Most flies see much faster than people. They can notice movement very quickly. One kind of fly, called the killer fly, sees six times faster than you do. Flies' eyes are amazing!

MIGHTY MOMENT

Killer flies use their eyes to hunt other flies. They can spot and catch a smaller fly in mid-air.

A CLOSER LOOK

Flies see more slowly when it's dark. Like you, their eyes need light to see.

What a fly sees helps it plan its escape. It turns its body in a safe direction before it takes off.

Simple eyes help a fly know which way is up or down. Many other insects, such as bees and dragonflies, also have simple eyes.

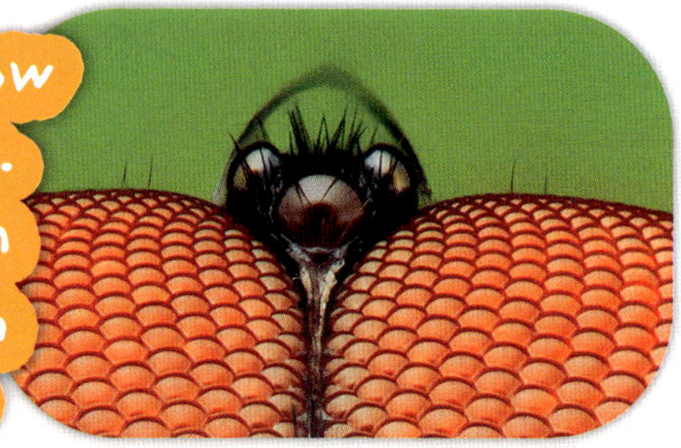

GLOSSARY

compound (kahm-pound) something formed by two or more parts

focus (foh-kuhs) to adjust the eyes to be able to see something clearly

lens (lenz) the clear part of the eye that light passes through

motion (moh-shuhn) movement

nerve (nurv) a bundle of fibers that carries signals between the rest of the body and the brain

senses (sen-sez) what a living creature uses to learn about its surroundings; seeing, hearing, taste, touch, and smell are the five senses

vision (vizh-uhn) the sense of sight

FURTHER READING

Golkar, Golriz. *All About Flies.* Jump! Inc., 2025.

Labrecque, Ellen. *Why Do Flies Like Gross Stuff?* Capstone, 2021.

ON THE INTERNET

Fly

https://kids.britannica.com/kids/article/fly/353138

Learn about the different kinds of flies, how big they are, and more with Britannica Kids.

True Flies, Including Mosquitos

https://biokids.umich.edu/critters/Diptera/

BioKids shares lots of info about flies, including where and how long they live.

INDEX